Useful but Unused –
Group Work in Europe

The European Foundation for the Improvement of Living and Working Conditions is an autonomous body of the European Union, created to assist the formulation of future policy on social and work-related matters. Further information can be found at the Foundation Web site at http://www.eurofound.ie/

Useful but Unused – Group Work in Europe

Findings from the EPOC Survey

Jos Benders
Fred Huijgen
Ulrich Pekruhl
Kevin P. O'Kelly

EUROPEAN FOUNDATION
for the Improvement of Living and Working Conditions

Wyattville Road, Loughlinstown, Co. Dublin, Ireland. Tel: +353 1 204 3100 Fax: +353 1 282 6456 E-mail: postmaster@eurofound.ie

Cataloguing data can be found at the end of this publication

Luxembourg: Office for Official Publications of the European Communities, 1999

ISBN 92-828-5568-6

© European Foundation for the Improvement of Living and Working Conditions, 1999

For rights of translation or reproduction, applications should be made to the Director, European Foundation for the Improvement of Living and Working Conditions, Wyattville Road, Loughlinstown, Co. Dublin, Ireland.

Printed in Ireland

The paper used in this publication is chlorine free and comes from managed forests in Northern Europe. For every tree felled, at least one new tree is planted.

Foreword

In recent years there has been a growing interest in new ways of organising work to make European enterprises more competitive on the global markets. As part of this new interest in organisational efficiency, direct participation arrangements such as total quality management, quality circles, team work and re-engineering have gained in popularity. The indications are that this new direct approach to employee involvement is of benefit not only to the organisation, but also to the workforce. For enterprises there is the increased efficient use of the human resource; for workers, the possibility of more meaningful jobs and a greater input into the workplace issues which directly affect their working lives. Unions and employers in Europe, in showing a greater interest in direct participation, are seeking to develop a social model which is unique to Europe and in contrast to the emergence of workplace models in other trading blocks.

In order to address these developments, the European Foundation for the Improvement of Living and Working Conditions initiated the EPOC Project (**E**mployee direct **P**articipation in **O**rganisational **C**hange). The objective of this project was to research the trend towards more direct participation in European enterprises, and to provide information which would feed into the debate between the social partners and the European Union institutions on the most appropriate form of work organisation for Europe.

So far the Foundation has produced six publications as part of this ongoing research project. The first report presented the conceptual framework of the EPOC project. The second publication was based on an analysis of research into the attitudes and understanding of the social partners in EU Member States, and the extent to which the application of direct participation can influence the humanisation of work, while at the same time increasing profitability.

The third report reviewed empirical research into direct participation in Europe, the United States and Japan and gives an overview of the existing knowledge on the topic. It examines the extent of the Japanese 'Toyota' model and contrasts it with the Scandinavian 'Volvo' model of work organisation, and has the most extensive literature review on this subject yet published in Europe.

Having carried out these research projects the Foundation paused to take stock, and a summary of the results so far was published in a booklet in 1996 which drew together all the knowledge EPOC had contributed to the debate. However, many questions were still unanswered and knowledge gaps remained. To fill these gaps the Foundation carried out a survey of managers, in ten Member States to ascertain the extent and nature of direct participation within their establishments. The responses to this survey provided a wealth of information and the first analysis of the survey results was published in 1997.

This first EPOC report on the survey results was a significant contribution to the policy debate around the European Commission's Green Paper *Partnership for a New Organisation of Work*. It provided, for the first time, detailed information on the extent of direct participation in its different forms; its economic and social impact; the attitudes of European management to it as a process for the efficient organisation of work, and the results of involving workers and their representatives in the process of change.

As a next step in the Foundation's contribution to the ongoing debate, a series of further analyses of the results of the survey were undertaken in 1998 under the headings of: equal opportunities in direct participation arrangements; the relationship between employment, organisational flexibility and innovation; direct participation in the social public services (this has been published); and, in this report, the nature and extent of group work in Europe.

Group work or group delegation, as it is defined in the EPOC workplace survey, is often considered in the scientific debate as a key component of direct participation. The objective of this form of employee involvement is to decentralise decision making on a range of agreed issues so as to increase workplace flexibility, fully utilise the skills and abilities of employees, and consequently improve the quality of working life.

In this study we found that group work as a form of work organisation is used in about a quarter of European workplaces. However, when its use was measured

Foreword

against an agreed set of criteria, it was found that there were very few 'team-based' workplaces in the survey sample – only 3.75% could be designated as such. Other important findings in this study are 1) that group work was introduced by management mainly for economic reasons – to increase efficiency and productivity – although in many cases social issues were also mentioned, generally in conjunction with economic motives; 2) that the range of decision-making rights was very limited; and 3) that management to a large extent controls the membership of the work teams and appoints the team leaders.

Clive Purkiss
Director

Eric Verborgh
Deputy Director

Contents

		Page
Foreword		v
Preface		xi
Chapter 1	**Introduction**	1
Chapter 2	**Methodology**	7
Chapter 3	**Group work: context and content**	17
Chapter 4	**Motives for and effects of group delegation**	35
Chapter 5	**Group work in an international perspective**	45
Chapter 6	**Teaming up for teams?**	51
References		57

Preface

In 1992 the European Foundation for the Improvement of Living and Working Conditions launched a major investigation into the nature and extent of direct participation and its role in organisational change, called the EPOC Project (**E**mployee direct **P**articipation in **O**rganisational **C**hange).

The first phase of the project included the development of a conceptual framework of direct participation to make it more accessible to empirical research (Geary and Sisson, 1994); a study of the understanding, attitudes and approaches of the social partners in the European Member States (Regalia, 1995); and an appraisal of the available research in the USA and Japan as well as at national level within the European Union (Fröhlich and Pekruhl, 1996). Also, as part of the project, a number of conferences and round tables of the social partners, governments and European Commission representatives were held.

The activity in the second phase has been the design, implementation and analysis of a representative postal survey of workplaces in ten EU countries, with the objective of helping to fill the information gap which was identified by the research in the first phase.

The EPOC Survey

The EPOC survey is the most comprehensive review of its kind into the nature and extent of direct employee participation. A standard questionnaire, translated with the help of industrial relations 'experts', was posted to a representative sample of workplaces in ten EU member countries: Denmark, France, Germany, Ireland, Italy, the Netherlands, Portugal, Spain, Sweden and the UK. Altogether, some 5,800 managers, from manufacturing and services, and from the public and the private sector, responded. The size threshold was 20 or 50 employees depending on size of the country. The respondent was either the general manager or the person he or she felt was the most appropriate. The main subject of the questions was the largest occupational group.

In keeping with the conceptual framework, the focus of the EPOC survey was on the two main forms of direct participation, which for the purposes of empirical enquiry can be defined as follows:

1. **Consultative participation** – management encourages employees to make their views known on work-related matters, but retains the right to take action or not.

2. **Delegative participation** – management gives employees increased discretion and responsibility to organise and do their jobs without reference back.

The essence of direct participation can be better understood by contrasting it with the other main forms of involvement and participation, such as:

- information disclosure
- financial participation
  - profit sharing
  - share ownership
- direct participation
  - consultative
  - delegative
- indirect or representative participation
  - joint consultation
  - co-determination
  - collective bargaining
  - board-level representation, such as worker directors

The key distinguishing features of direct participation are consultation and delegation. This is in contrast to financial participation, i.e. profit sharing and share ownership which might involve consultation or delegation. With indirect or representative participation, where workers are involved through their elected representatives, the word 'indirect' is key: whereas indirect participation takes place through the intermediary of representative bodies, such as works councils or trade unions, direct participation involves employees themselves immediately in the decision-making process.

Both consultation and delegative participation can involve individual employees or groups of employees. The two forms of consultative participation can be further subdivided. Individual consultation can be 'face-to-face' or at 'arms length'; group consultation can involve temporary or permanent groups. This gives us six forms of direct participation regardless of the particular labels applied. The six forms are set out below, together with examples of relevant practices from the research review and round-table discussions. The EPOC survey questionnaire was structured around these six forms.

The main forms of direct participation are:

- individual consultation
  'face-to-face': arrangements involving discussions between the individual employee and his/her immediate manager, such as regular performance reviews, regular training and development reviews and '360 degree' appraisal;

  'arms-length': arrangements which allow individual employees to express their views through a 'third party', such as a 'speak-up' scheme with 'counsellor' or 'ombudsman', or through attitude surveys and suggestion schemes

- group consultation
  'temporary' groups: groups of employees who come together for a specific purpose and for a limited period of time, e.g. 'project groups' or 'task forces'

  'permanent' groups: groups of employees that discuss various work related topics on an ongoing basis, such as quality circles

- individual delegation
  individual employees are granted extended rights and responsibilities to carry out their work without constant reference back to managers – sometimes known as 'job enrichment'

- group delegation
  rights and responsibilities are granted to groups of employees to carry out their common tasks without constant reference back to managers – most often known as 'group work'.

The questionnaire also asked about a range of other issues, such as the other management initiatives which had been undertaken in the workplace. These included questions about changes in levels of employment, economic performances and the scope and intensity of the various forms of direct participation. The questionnaire is reproduced in the first survey report published by the Foundation (EPOC Research Group, 1997).

The third phase of the EPOC project included further detailed analysis of the survey results on a number of important topics for the future organisation of work within the European Union. This report is one of these studies and its focus is on the nature and extent of group delegation, or 'group work', in the ten countries.

We would like to acknowledge the useful comments of David Buchanan, Leicester Business School, De Montfort University, UK, on the draft of this report.

Jos Benders, Nijmegen Business School, Netherlands
Fred Huijgen, Nijmegen Business School, Netherlands
Ulrich Pekruhl, Institut Arbeit und Technik, Germany
Kevin P. O'Kelly, European Foundation for the Improvement of Living and Working Conditions

Chapter 1　Introduction

Group work: a persistent concern

Group work is even older than the phenomenon of the 'formal organisation' – one can easily imagine bands of hunters chasing mammoths. These animals were too large for individual hunters, and the bands more than likely developed routines to trap, kill and slaughter their prey. If true, the claim that the extinction of mammoths was caused by large-scale hunting could even be interpreted as early proof of the success of group work. Forms of cooperating in groups emerged and developed spontaneously all over the world. Wherever people work together in groups to achieve a common task, the work has to be divided over the group's members and coordinated between them. Hence, in terms of an empirical phenomenon, the topic of this report is considerably older than the roads to Rome.

Nevertheless, in the present public and scientific debate group work has become a (if not the) focal point of attention. The reason for this widespread interest lies in the promises group work embodies: improved economic performance coinciding with more rewarding work. As such, group work is a reaction against the dysfunctions of a high division of labour within organisations. Strongly fragmented organisations are hard to manage, have difficulties in reacting to environmental changes, and lead to the alienation of workers and underutilisation of their competence. The new orthodoxy for modern managers has become a flat organisation, made up of self-directed teams. It seems that in the 1990s this remedy is prescribed to cure the ills of the apparently still prevailing fragmented organisation. But is the prescription followed?

The question becomes more pressing considering that the 'group work medicine' has frequently been prescribed in the course of the last fifty years or so (Beyerlein, 1999). A 1951 article on the 'longwall method of coal-getting' (Trist and Bamforth, 1951) is often mentioned as the beginning of theorising about group work, or at least of the sociotechnical research tradition. Trist and Bamforth stressed the importance of the 'wholeness' of the work process, 'responsible autonomy' in the group, and the 'multiplicity of skills of the individual' group member. Subsequently, theoretical and empirical studies at the London-based Tavistock Institute became a source of inspiration for researchers elsewhere in Europe (Van Eijnatten, 1993). All manifestations of such sociotechnical teams can be subsumed under a definition, such as:

> a group of workers, generally between four and 20 persons, responsible for a rounded-off part of the production process, and entitled to take certain decisions autonomously.

The idea of 'autonomous work teams' was disseminated under a gamut of different labels. In different periods and different countries, adjectives such as autonomous, semi-autonomous, self-directed, high-performing, and self-managed were used in combination with substantives like 'teams', 'groups' and 'work units'. European traditions on teamwork have all directly or indirectly been informed by the original sociotechnical notion of 'autonomous work groups'. The 'embrace' of teamworking, as Buchanan (1998) calls it, was enduring.

Whereas academic debates on the exact theoretical meaning and operation of 'autonomy' have not yet resulted in consensus, the notion remains a powerful ideal or *leitmotiv* in the practice of work and organisation design, even though its actual realisation is almost always incomplete. 'More an ambition than reality', De Sitter calls it (1998: 292), yet the challenge in designing work groups is to try to match the reality as closely to the ideal as possible.

In efforts to resolve the Babylonic confusion that results from the gamut of available theoretical notions and practical experiences, academic authors have reserved some of these combinations for particular well-delineated forms of work teams. Yet such fine academic distinctions tend to get lost in the world of practitioners, a process that was and is only accelerated with the apparently increasing popularity of teams. In a way, teams have become a victim of their own success. As Czarniawska and Joerges (1996) aptly put it, 'ideas travel in time and space'.

Writings about teams contain ideas, but these are often abstract and, indeed, must be so to allow for broad applicability. Yet at the same time, this means that there are different interpretations about what teams 'really are'. In addition, peculiarities play a role in every particular case where teamwork is implemented. All ideas and notions need to be put into a context. Work teams have been and are implemented in a variety of settings, which partly determine the end result. Many debates on teamwork concentrate on a very specific production environment, namely the final assembly of passenger cars. The short-cyclic nature of working at assembly lines is an important impediment to realising the autonomy ideal. Other organisational settings such as nursing, construction and machine building generally lend themselves far better to the realisation of socio technically-inspired teamwork. Practical experiences with teams in all such environments are discussed, often informally between those engaged or interested in using the generic idea, but sometimes formally through publications in the business and/or academic press. Through various communication channels, practical experiences are fed back which in turn transform notions about what teams are. In their turn, these transformed notions become the ideas upon which to act. In this perspective teams' popularity inevitably leads to building a Babylonic tower.

That, however, does not mean that academics' efforts to develop categories of teams are useless. On the contrary, such categories are necessary to come to grips with the complex empirical reality and may also serve as models which can inspire practitioners. A much used way to distinguish forms of teams is dichotomies between what has been labeled 'sociotechnical'/'Swedish'/ 'Scandinavian' teams on the one hand and 'lean'/'Japanese'/'Toyotist' teams on the other. Especially during the 1980s, 'teams' were assigned a crucial role in explaining the strong performance of Japanese manufacturers; for instance, in a best-selling book on the global automotive industry it is stated that: 'it is the dynamic work team that emerges as the heart of the lean factory' (Womack, Jones and Roos, 1991: 99).

Articles in the business press in which teams were linked to superior performance probably paved the way for the breakthrough of teams in practice. Until roughly the late 1980s teamwork was an important topic in academic literature, but apart from pilot projects and the odd forerunner organisation, in practice 'teams' failed to make the breakthrough. This seems to change, however, with the advent of the 'Japanese team', but at the same time academics started issuing warnings, that sociotechnically-inspired teams are different from the Japanese work organisation which has also been called 'team'. Table 1.1

contains the dichotomy which was used in the second phase of the EPOC project, which focuses on a review of empirical literature.

Table 1.1 *Types of group work*

dimensions	Scandinavian	Toyota/lean production
membership	voluntary	mandatory
selection of group members	by the group	by management
selection of group leader	by the group	by management
qualifications	mixed	generalists
reward	skill dependent	uniform (seniority)
task	complex	simple
technology	independent of pace	dependent on pace
autonomy	large	narrow
internal division of labour	voluntary	largely prescribed

Source: EPOC Research Group, 1997: 58.

Unfortunately, the richness of insights that can be derived from reviewing existing sources cannot, for obvious economic and practical reasons, be duplicated in a survey such as the third phase of the EPOC project. In addition, group work is only one of several forms of direct participation which were included in the survey. Hence, the available data do not allow the inclusion of all the dimensions listed in Table 1.1. In other words, in this secondary analysis it is not possible to assess to what extent 'Toyotist' and 'Scandinavian' teams are found in European practice. The good news, however, is that the EPOC survey contained data about what is generally seen as the most essential difference between the two forms of team: the distribution of decision rights. Hence we decided to refocus and to substitute the labels 'Scandinavian' and 'Toyotist' by more precise terms that do justice to the data available. The terminology and methodological details are explained in Chapter 2. It should be noted however that, although the EPOC survey by no means tackles all the interesting questions, this is nevertheless the first empirical, cross-national study on the spread of teamworking in Europe. That makes it more than worthwhile to analyse the EPOC survey data on what the findings are in relation to 'teams in Europe'.

The plan of the report

The next chapter describes the methodology of the survey and the statistical techniques used in the report. Chapter 3 deals with the context and content of 'group delegation' and 'group work' respectively (see p. 13 for a discussion on how both are related). Chapter 4 focuses on motives for and reported effects of implementing group delegation. In Chapter 5 the diffusion of group delegation is investigated in a cross-national perspective. Chapter 6, finally, contains the conclusions and some policy recommendations.

Chapter 2   Methodology

This report focuses on group delegation and draws on data collected in the EPOC establishment survey in 1996. This chapter introduces the survey, sets out the statistical definition of group delegation used in the report and gives the basic characteristics of the workplaces with group work.

The EPOC survey

Respondents

The EPOC survey was planned to be representative of workplaces in as many countries as the budget would reasonably allow, taking into account a range of different populations and geographical positions. The ten countries finally chosen were: Denmark, France, Germany, Ireland, Italy, the Netherlands, Portugal, Spain, Sweden and the UK. The choice of the workplace as the level and the general manager as the immediate target is explained by the overall aim of the survey, which was to gather as much data as possible about what was happening in practice. A survey directed at higher levels in the organisation was unlikely to have produced such information and there was some concern that small workplaces in particular might not have a personnel manager. In any event, the general manager was invited to complete the questionnaire him/herself or to pass it on to the manager most capable of doing so.

In targeting managers only, and not employees or their representatives as well, the EPOC survey is open to the criticism that its results are one sided. Much as the EPOC Research Group would like to have included employee representatives especially in the survey, the costs of doing so proved to be prohibitive. In many workplaces it would have been necessary to get a response from more than one employee representative and in some countries there would also have been enormous complexity in identifying the most appropriate respondent(s).

The omission of employee respondents is perhaps not as much of a weakness as it might at first appear, however. The main objective of the EPOC survey was to establish the nature and extent of direct participation. The experience of the Foundation's survey on *Workplace Involvement in Technological Innovation in the European Community* (Fröhlich, Gill and Krieger 1993), which involved responses from almost 4,000 employee representatives as well as from an identical number of managers, showed a high consensus about factual issues between both groups of workplace respondents. Also, a unique feature of the EPOC survey was that it did not simply ask about the incidence of direct participation, which managers might have been tempted to exaggerate. Questions designed to estimate the coverage, scope and intensity of the processes involved helped to ensure a balanced picture.

Organisation of the survey

The questionnaire, which is reproduced in full in the first report on the survey analysis (EFILWC[1], 1997), was initially drawn up in English by members of the research group, with the help of a team from the Industrial Relations Research Unit at the University of Warwick, and translated by themselves and trusted experts into the other languages. Tenders to administer it were invited in the Official Journal of the European Union in September 1995. In December 1995, INTOMART, representing GfK Europe, and based in Hilversum (the Netherlands), was commissioned to do the job. With INTOMART's help, the questionnaire was pre-tested in the ten countries in the winter of 1995 and the spring of 1996.

Details of the main survey

The gross sample of workplaces, drawn up by the national GfK members, differed for the ten countries according to population size, the number of employees in industry and services, and the number of workplaces with 20 or more employees (for the smaller and medium-sized countries) and 50 or more employees (for the larger ones). For the larger countries (France, Germany, Italy, Spain, the UK) the gross sample was 5,000 workplaces; for the medium

---

[1]European Foundation for the Improvement of Living and Working Conditions.

countries (Denmark, the Netherlands and Sweden) 2,500 and for the smaller countries (Ireland and Portugal) 1,000.

The mailing was carried out in two full waves, including the questionnaire and the accompanying letter, followed by one additional reminder letter. The first questionnaires were mailed in the beginning of June 1996. Because of the varying times of summer holidays, an additional mailing was carried out in those countries where the response rate was below 20 per cent: France, Germany, Italy, the Netherlands, Spain and the United Kingdom. This additional mailing was carried out in October 1996, focused on certain sectors, and was accompanied by an extra letter of recommendation.

Each of the national GfK member institutions drew up the final gross samples for their respective countries. Table 2.1 holds the final gross sample figures, the net samples (gross sample minus 'return to sender'), the number of returned questionnaires and the response rate per country. The response rate in column 4 is based on columns 2 and 3.

From the gross sample of 33,427 questionnaires, 849 (2.5 per cent) were returned to sender by the different postal services either because the address was wrong or unknown, or the addressee had moved to an unknown address, or the company had ceased to exist altogether. By 15 November 1996, 5,786 questionnaires had been returned and it was on the basis of these that the data analysis took place.

In data analysis, the remaining sample distortions regarding sector and size of the workplace were weighted for each sector/size cell to reflect the original research universe. The sample distortions between countries were corrected by a weighting factor that accounted for the number of employees represented in the data set for each country and the overall size of the workforce in that country.

Assessment of the response

The number of explicit refusals was very low: only about 400 potential respondents indicated that they were not willing to cooperate. On the basis of remarks made by respondents either on the telephone or in the questionnaire, direct participation was regarded as a subject of some importance. In addition, a large number of respondents (47 per cent) responded positively to the question asking if they would like to receive a summary of the results.

Table 2.1 *Sample sizes and questionnaire returns*

	gross sample (absolute nos)	net sample (absolute nos)	questionnaire returns (absolute nos)	response %
Denmark	2,600	2,535	674	26.6
France	5,028	4,870	598	12.3
Germany	4,954	4,887	826	16.9
Ireland	1,000	984	382	38.8
Italy	3,949	3,849	499	13.0
Netherlands	2,386	2,303	505	21.9
Portugal	1,000	996	298	29.9
Spain	5,062	4,872	460	9.4
Sweden	2,448	2,401	732	30.5
United Kingdom	5,000	4,881	812	16.6
Total	33,427	32,578	5,786	17.8

An overall return rate of 18 per cent was not as high as the Research Group hoped for. It is not out of line, however, with comparable cross-national postal surveys of Price Waterhouse Cranfield (PWC) (Brewster and Hegewisch, 1994) and Harzing (1997). The overall return rates of usable questionnaires were 17 and 20 per cent respectively, which is close to the EPOC response rate. Table 2.2 compares the results of the three surveys in detail.

Table 2.2 *EPOC response rates compared to two other cross-national postal surveys*

	EPOC %	Harzing %	PWC %
Denmark	27	42	19
France	12	14	15
Germany	17	16	15
Ireland	39	31	(not in sample)
Italy	13	24	10
Netherlands	22	27	19
Portugal	30	(not in sample)	(not in sample)
Spain	9	16	14
Sweden	31	20	42
United Kingdom	17	19	19
Average	18	23	17

The EPOC response rate for Spain was clearly below the Harzing and PWC equivalents. The response rates for the three large countries, France, Germany and the United Kingdom, are about the same in all three surveys. EPOC's response rates in Denmark, Italy, the Netherlands and Sweden are in between those of both reference studies. The Irish response rate in the EPOC survey is clearly very high. For Portugal, no comparable data are available.

Additional information from similar national surveys is also instructive:

- a German national postal survey (Lay, Dreher and Kinkel, 1996) on the same topic in the production sector had an identical response rate to that of the EPOC survey: 18 per cent;
- an earlier Dutch national postal survey on a similar topic (Muffels, Heinen and van Mil 1982) had a return rate of 28 per cent which is higher than that of the EPOC survey (22 per cent);
- the EPOC survey's response rate for Portugal (30 per cent) is quite high. A similar postal survey carried out by Kovacs, Cerdeira and Moniz (1992) had a return rate of 12 per cent;
- high return rates seem to be the norm in Sweden. The EPOC rate for this country (31 per cent) is in between that of the PWC survey (42 per cent) and Harzing's study (20 per cent), but it approaches the figure (34 per cent) of a national postal survey on flexible organisations (NUTEK 1996).

Thus, with the exception of Portugal, the return rates for Germany and Sweden data were not out of line with what appears to be the norm for these countries. Taking two further cross-national studies, the rates for France, the United Kingdom and Spain in particular seem to be somewhat below expectations. The account is less clear for Denmark, Italy, the Netherlands and Sweden: EPOC's response is in between those of PWC and Harzing.

Comparable though it may be, an 18 per cent overall return rate raises the question of how far the estimated parameters of interest suffer from a probability bias. In other words, are the workplaces with direct participation under represented or over represented in the EPOC results? Are the data negatively or positively biased? This issue was investigated in a project undertaken by NUTEK, dealing with the spread and functioning of 'flexible organisations' in Sweden in preparation for the G7 summit in France in early summer 1996. The representative survey had a response rate of 34 per cent, which is very close to that of the EPOC survey for Sweden. To evaluate the representative of the data, telephone follow-ups were made to try to establish the degree of flexibility in non-respondent organisations. The verdict was that 'the non-response sample seems to have a larger proportion of workplaces defined as a flexible work organisation' as compared to the respondents (NUTEK, 1996:

195, 198). In other words, the survey results underestimated the extent of flexible organisations in Sweden.

It does not necessarily follow that the same is true of the EPOC results. It simply suggests that under representation is a possibility, as is over representation. There is no reason to believe that the EPOC results are biased one way or the other.

The concept of the 'largest occupational group'

The EPOC survey targeted the **largest occupational group** (the 'largest number of non-managerial employees at this workplace', in the precise words of the questionnaire). This was done for two reasons: to reduce the complexity of answers required of respondents; and to ensure that answers were as characteristic of as many employees as possible. Inevitably, however, focusing on the largest occupational group (or LOG) raises questions about the relationship between these employees and the workforce as a whole. Especially important when the issue of employment is involved is whether or not it is possible to generalise from the experience of the LOG to the total workforce.

The detailed analysis of the ratio between the LOG and the total number of employees in Table 2.3 shows that, on average, the number of employees in the former is about 63 per cent (mean) of the latter and the most frequent ratio (mode) is two thirds (67 per cent). Overall, in 70 per cent of cases, the LOG stood for 50 per cent or more of the establishments' workforce, and in 30 per cent it represented 76 to 100 percent of it. Only in five per cent of cases did the LOG account for 25 percent or less of the total number of employees. In short, it seems not unreasonable to generalise from the experience of the LOG to the total number of employees.

Table 2.3 *The ratio of the number of employees in the largest occupational group to the total number of employees*

Mean	62%
Mode	67%
0 – 25%	5%
25 – 50%	25%
50 – 75%	40%
75 – 100%	30%
Total	100%

Terms and definitions

As already stated in the preface (p. xiii), 'group delegation' is described in the EPOC study as follows:

> rights and responsibilities are granted to groups of employees to carry out their common tasks without constant reference back to managers – most often known as 'group work' (EPOC Research Group, 1997: 18).

In the questionnaire, delegative participation was described as:

> management gives non-managerial employees in the largest occupational group at workplace level increased responsibility to organise and do their jobs without reference back (**decision making**).

In this context a central question seeks to assess whether or not group delegation was practised:

> Has the management given to formally introduced GROUPS the right to make DECISIONS on how their work is performed on a GROUP basis without reference to immediate managers for *one or more* of the following:
>
> – allocation of work
> – scheduling of work
> – quality of work
> – time keeping
> – attendance and absence control
> – job rotation
> – coordination of work with other internal groups
> – improving work processes.

The total number of positive answers can range from a minimum of one to a maximum of eight. This number was used to assess the **intensity** of group delegation, which can be seen as an indicator of group autonomy. That the inclusion of autonomy builds on sociotechnically-informed traditions in work and organisation design, which over the years were key to conceptual and practical developments in several European countries, should be noted.

Data on the proportion of employees in the largest occupational group involved in group delegation were used to select the organisations that apply group delegation on a broad scale. Therefore, we excluded establishments where group delegation was introduced only on a pilot basis, or where the approach only diffused to a limited number of employees. Table 2.1 gives an overview of this so-called 'coverage', e.g. the proportion of employees involved in group decision making.

Table 2.4 *Coverage of group delegation*

coverage	number of cases	valid percentage
0 – 9 %	241	17.2
10 – 19 %	283	20.1
20 – 29 %	190	13.5
30 – 39 %	69	4.9
40 – 49 %	89	6.3
50 – 59 %	30	2.1
60 – 69 %	41	2.9
70 – 79 %	66	4.7
80 – 89 %	24 *462*	1.7
90 – 100 %	372	26.5
Total	1,405	100

To be able to estimate the effects of group work, we are particularly interested in those workplaces in which group delegation is the dominant pattern of work organisation. Moreover, in these companies the word 'group' must be more than merely a label. In other words, the group must be assigned a minimum degree of discretion. Thus, in order to qualify as a 'team-based' workplace, two criteria have to be met:

1. an intensity of at least four decision rights; and
2. a coverage of at least 70 percent.

As can be inferred from Table 2.4, the latter applies to 462 workplaces. Applying the first criterion to these 462 cases leaves 217 cases to be used in analyses which would characterise 'team-based' workplaces (or organisations). As these analyses require a breakdown of these initial 217 cases, 'small-numbers' problems easily occur which constrain the possibilities for conducting in-depth analyses of some issues of theoretical interest.

To learn whether these team-based workplaces differ greatly from those forms of work organisation in which groups are not dominant, or even marginal, we put the data in perspective. To do so, the 'team-based' workplaces are compared to relevant reference groups. The workplaces with group delegation are split into three subcategories:

- 'team-based' organisations;
- 'medium GD'
- 'weak GD'.

Methodology

Figure 2.1 depicts graphically how these three subcategories relate to each other.

Figure 2.1 *The three group delegation (GD) subcategories*

		intensity (number of decision rights)	
		1 - 3	4 - 8
coverage (percentage)	0 – 29	weak GD	
	30 – 69		medium GD
	70 -100		team-based

As shown in Figure 2.1, the weak GD cases are located in the upper left corner, whereas the team-based cases can be found in the lower right corner. The subcategory 'medium GD' is a rest category, and its composition in somewhat heterogeneous.

Table 2.5 lists the criteria, and the number of cases in each of the three subcategories.

Table 2.5: *Criteria for the three group delegation (GD) subcategories*

category	team-based organisations	medium GD	weak GD
criteria	Coverage at least 70 per cent. Intensity at least four decision rights.	Cases not satisfying criteria for either 'weak GD' or 'team-based'.	Coverage less than 30 per cent. Intensity less than four decision rights.
number of cases	217	720	467

Where the data are available, these GD subcategories are also compared to workplaces without DP and/or workplaces with forms of DP other than group delegation ('other DP').

Methodology

The breakdown by GD categories lead to a substantial reduction in the usable response. Specifically, 3,528 respondents answered that they had group delegation in place, yet of these only 1,887 specified the decision rights, whereas 1,748 respondents gave data about the coverage. For 1,403 establishments data about both variables are available. To avoid speculation and assure the reliability of our findings, we chose not to include the cases with missing data. One consequence of this cautious attitude is that the data on the incidence of group work should be considered as minima.

Chapter 3 Group Work: Context and Content

In this chapter, the available EPOC data on group delegation are presented in as far as they concern:

1. the organisational context; and
2. characteristics of the teams.

The latter are subdivided into the distribution of decision rights, the composition of teams, training, payment systems, and improvement activities. The chapter ends with a summary of the conclusions.

To place the data on group delegation into the perspective of the EPOC survey, it should be mentioned that of the 5,786 responding organisations, 19% stated that they did not use any form of direct participation, 55% use individual consultation, 54% use individual delegation, 51% have group consultation and 33% group delegation.

At first glance, this seems to indicate that direct participation (DP) is quite common at European workplaces. However, an in-depth analysis of the data (EPOC Research Group, 1997) reveals that in most cases DP is very limited: very few decision-making rights are given to the workforce and there are also very few occasions when management consults with employees. The above data should be interpreted, as some elements of direct participation can be found in the vast majority of European workplaces, but concepts which could be labelled as 'participative management' are only applied in a minority of organisations. This general remark also holds for the case of group delegation. Taking into account the strict criteria for handling the missing answers, in the last chapter only 217 workplaces were characterised as 'team-based'. This amounts to less than 4 per cent of all workplaces in the survey sample. Hence, despite the long-standing attention given to group work in managerial and academic literature, its rate of diffusion is still low.

Contextual characteristics

The abundant amount of literature on group work has one important bias. If group work in the automotive industry is not the topic itself, discussions still tend to be on this particular industry. Most attention in these discussions is paid to the most labour-intensive part of the production processes, namely final assembly. It is easy to understand the existence of these biases for a range of reasons:

1. The product appeals to many.
2. Most car plants are large and thus there is much to be seen and investigated.
3. The factories are also the core of industrial networks within which a considerable amount of knowledge transfer takes place. Ever since the moving assembly line was first applied at Ford the automotive industry was looked upon for 'best practices'.
4. Final assembly is a problematic area – working at assembly lines is a tough job which requires that management find ways of keeping assembly workers motivated.

The drawback to this attention on final car assembly is that the production environment has rather specific characteristics. For several years large numbers of fairly identical products are made in short-cyclic production. This type of production is generally controlled in detail. Engineers design machinery that allows little latitude for workers and, in addition, tight standard operating procedures are devised to prescribe assemblers' jobs. One must realise that most other production environments are more suited to allowing group members a certain level of autonomy, not only because there are less prescriptions but also because these are less detailed.

The 'final car assembly'-bias may create the impression that the automotive industry is the leading sector using teamwork. Unfortunately, the EPOC survey cannot provide conclusive evidence about the relative position of the automotive industry as there are only data available for manufacturing industries in general.

Yet, as shown in Table 3.1 and 3.2, manufacturing industries are not the leading users of group delegation.

Table 3.1 *The incidence of DP and different forms of GD by sector*
 (N = 5303; row percentages)

	manufacturing	construction	trade	services	non-profit
non-DP	41	11	18	16	14
other DP	38	6	19	16	21
weak GD	37	11	23	14	15
medium GD	33	5	22	17	23
team-based	31	3	7	20	39
Total	38	7	19	16	21

The bottom line of Table 3.1 shows the sectoral division of the responses. For example, 38 % of all respondents are from the manufacturing sector. Comparing the importance of the sectors with the incidence of direct participation in general, and group delegation in particular, it shows that the non-profit sector is clearly leading, followed by service industries. 39% of all cases of 'team-based workplaces' can be found in non-profit organisations whereas these form only 21% of all respondents (the data for services are 20% and 16%, respectively). With 31% of team-based workplaces, manufacturing scores below the 38% with which the sector is represented in the response set. Indeed, it is the only sector in which the scores for the different forms of GD are persistently below the overall representation, although scores are low as well in trade and construction. These data suggest that researchers should look at non-profit rather than manufacturing organisations if they want to find exemplars of team-based work.

In Table 3.2, the same data are presented, but now in terms of the occurrence of direct participation and group delegation within the sectors.

The data in Table 3.2 confirms the findings that non-profit organisations are leading and that manufacturing industries are lagging behind, although the differences appear less pronounced. The exception is the high occurrence of team-based organisations in the non-profit sector, which, with 8%, is twice the average.

Table 3.2 *The incidence of DP and different forms of GD by sector*
(N = 5303; column percentages)

	manufacturing	construction	trade	services	non-profit	Total
non-DP	23	32	19	20	14	21
other DP	53	43	53	52	56	53
weak GD	9	13	10	7	7	9
medium GD	12	10	16	15	15	14
team-based	3	2	1	5	8	4

These data were checked for size and ownership (domestic EU or non-EU owned), but these did not make any difference.

Possibly the incidence of group delegation has to do with labour intensity. The underlying reason is that the higher the labour intensity, the more critical the effective utilisation of human resources becomes, and hence the more likely that managers will deploy contemporary 'best practices', as work teams can be considered in the late 1990s. Table 3.3 presents data on the relationship between the proportion of labour costs (as percentage of the cost price) and the use of direct participation and group delegation.

Table 3.3 *The incidence of DP and different forms of GD by proportion of labour costs*
(N = 4690; row percentages)

	less than 25%	25% to 49%	50% to 74%	75% and more
non-DP	28	43	17	13
other DP	24	40	24	12
weak GD	20	54	15	11
medium GD	22	40	22	15
team-based	17	29	33	22

Overall, the relationship between the proportion of labour costs and the occurrence of (forms of) direct participation is weak, but there is one notable exception: when labour costs are high, there are indeed more team-based organisations. Twenty-two per cent of all team-based organisations are found when labour costs make up 75% or more of total costs and another 33% when labour costs make up between 50% and 75%. However, as shown in Table 3.4, there is a sectoral effect.

Non-profit (and service) organisations are more labour-intensive than organisations in the other sectors and, as demonstrated in Tables 3.1 and 3.2, it is in these sectors that group delegation is used more intensively. A further analysis revealed that both the sector and the percentage of labour costs have an effect on the form of GD, and that the combined effect is strongest.

Table 3.4 *Sector by proportion of labour costs (N = 5106; row percentages)*

	less than 25%	25% to 49%	50% to 74%	75% and more
manufacturing	31	55	11	3
construction	18	53	18	11
trade	40	32	24	4
services	11	35	36	19
non-profit	11	21	33	36

Another matter of concern is whether GD is an isolated concept of employee participation or whether it is combined with other DP forms. The hypothesis is that team-based workplaces, which is considered the ultimate application of participative patterns of work organisation, are also open for other forms of employee involvement. This hypothesis is proved by the data, as shown in Table 3.5.

Table 3.5 *Different forms of GD by number of DP forms applied (N = 1403; row percentages)*

	1 form (only GD)	2 forms	3 forms	4 forms
weak GD	7	14	36	43
medium GD	1	18	28	53
team-based	2	14	21	63

The data in Table 3.5 show that three forms of direct participation are found together in 63% of the team-based workplaces, i.e. individual consultation, individual delegation, and group delegation. The other two categories of GD are also frequently applied in parallel with other DP forms, although the effect is less marked the 'lower' the GD-category (respectively 43% for weak GD, and 53% for medium GD).

This raises the issue of how important the respondents find the different forms of DP.

Table 3.6 shows that although group delegation is felt to be more important by those respondents in whose organisations it is applied, the respondents in general find group consultation to be more important. In the case of weak and medium GD, they also think that individual consultation is more important than group delegation. Only in team-based organisations is group delegation found to be more important than individual consultation.

Table 3.6 *Workplaces with other DP and different forms of GD workplaces by form of DP ranked by importance at the workplace (N = 2543; row percentages)*

	individual consultation	group consultation	individual delegation	group delegation
other DP	45	40	11	4
weak GD	32	43	5	20
medium GD	27	43	8	22
team-based	23	42	4	31

Obviously these data can be interpreted in different ways. On the one hand, one can state that the respondents prefer consultation over (group) delegation. This may signal an unwillingness to delegate, and/or management's inclination to keep close control of production environments, and/or the feeling that employees are not (yet?) sufficiently capable of taking decisions by themselves. On the other hand, respondents with experience of group delegation favour that form more than those with no experience of it.

As will be shown below, in almost all cases GD goes together with group consultation. They are two sides of the same coin. Consequently, it is hard to separate the two forms, let alone to decide which is the most important one.

The differences in the industrial relations systems in the ten countries investigated make it difficult to arrive at reliable conclusions about the relationships between the involvement of employee representatives in the introduction of group work and group work itself. Possibly relevant aspects include union membership; the forms of employee representation, such as unions, works' councils and shop stewards, and the presence of collective labour agreements. The problem is that where such aspects are essential in one country, they may be simply non-existent in others. Analysing such effects by (groups of fairly homogeneous) countries is hindered by small-numbers problems. What can be said at a rather high level of abstraction, however, is that there is a positive correlation between the intensity of the involvement of employee representatives in introducing group work and the incidence of the different GD forms. Most notably, in the case of team-based establishments there is far more negotiation/joint decision making (the heaviest level of involvement distinguished in the EPOC survey) than with the other forms.

The distribution of decision rights

As discussed in the introduction to this report, the notion of 'autonomy' features as an ideal to be achieved in designing self-managed work teams. The EPOC survey included a question that asked on which of the following eight topics the group was given the right to decide:

- allocation of work
- scheduling of work
- quality of work
- time keeping
- attendance and absence control
- job rotation
- coordination of work with other internal groups
- improving work processes.

The answers to this question were used to construct the three subcategories – weak GD, medium GD and team-based workplaces – based on the number of decision rights which groups have. Table 3.7 contains data about the extent to which groups can decide about the separate topics.

As shown in the bottom line of Table 3.7, in 53% of the organisations with GD, groups have the right to schedule their own work and to improve work processes. In slightly fewer organisations, namely 47%, groups allocate work themselves. Around 40% of all groups make decisions on the quality of work, time keeping, and coordinating with other groups. Only a few groups decide about attendance and job rotation.

Obviously there are substantial differences between the three subcategories of GD organisations. Because the number of decision rights was used to make the distribution into these three categories in the first place, these differences must necessarily surface in Table 3.7.

Nevertheless, it is interesting to take a closer look at possible patterns. One finding is that for all subcategories there are roughly three groups of decision rights, in the following descending order:

1. allocation of work, scheduling of work and improving work processes;
2. quality of work, time keeping and coordination; and
3. attendance and absence control and job rotation.

Table 3.7 *Different forms of GD by decision rights (N = 1403, percentages)*

	allocation of work	scheduling	quality of work	time keeping	attendance and absence control	job rotation	coordinating work with other groups	improving work processes
weak GD	27	34	23	31	14	15	27	38
medium GD	52	58	44	45	32	29	41	57
team-based	77	76	60	56	51	38	57	75
% of total	47	53	40	42	29	26	39	53

Groups' decision rights most often concern regulating tasks which are closely linked to their operational tasks – planning and improving work. Apparently management is less inclined to delegate controlling activities, and in only a minority of cases are groups entitled to take decisions on attendance and absenteeism (29%). More often, groups have decision rights with respect to the quality of work (40%), time keeping (42%) and coordination with other groups (39%).

Given that teamwork is often associated with broadly deployable workers, i.e. that team members should be able to carry out different jobs within the team, it comes as a surprise that in only 26% of all GD organisations do groups take decisions on job rotation. This may have to do with the fact that few organisations have adopted job rotation explicitly as a strategic initiative: only 13% of all organisations with GD have done so. Table 3.8 contains data on the use of job rotation as a strategic initiative, and on the group's right to decide about job rotation in those cases where it is adopted as a strategic initiative. As can be seen, job rotation is applied more often the 'higher' the GD category, and more importantly, groups are more often assigned the right to decide about job rotation themselves. In team-based organisations the score is 85%.

Table 3.8 *Different GD forms by job rotation adopted as a strategic initiative, and the right of the group to decide about job rotation (N = 1402; percentages)*

	job rotation is strategic initiative	job rotation is strategic initiative and group decides about it
weak GD	11	21
medium GD	12	41
team-based	18	85

Group composition

As in the first discussions on teamwork, the issues of who decides on group membership and group leadership have featured prominently. Table 3.9 contains

Group Work: Context and Content

data on whether management, the group, or both decide who is to be a group member.

Table 3.9 *Different forms of GD by who decides on group membership (N = 1329; row percentages)*

	management	both	group
weak GD	49	40	11
medium GD	36	44	20
team-based	32	53	15

The choice of team members is most often a joint decision of management and the group, although in the case of weak GD, management is most likely to take the decision on its own. Also, with medium GD and team-based organisations, managers feature prominently as sole decision makers. For all GD forms, only in a minority of cases is the group autonomous in deciding what person(s) will be members.

Team leadership has always been a prominent and much contested issue in the literature on teams. According to the more radical sociotechnical notions, team members should decide themselves who is to join and who is to be team leader, or indeed if there is to be a leader at all. However, in practice this preference appears to be realised only to a limited extent. Team leaders with decision-making powers occur in transitory phases towards 'real teams', but more often the leaderless form appears to be dismissed as a utopian ideal. In stark contrast to that, the Japanese work unit is characterised by a strong leader (Dore, 1973; Nomura and Jürgens, 1995). This leading position has been translated into English as 'subforeman' or 'foreman', and also as 'team leader'. Given the importance attached to team leadership, it is interesting to have a look at what the EPOC data say on this issue.

Table 3.10 *Different forms of GD by team leadership (N = 1307; row percentages)*

	team leaders in all groups	team leaders in some groups	no team leader
weak GD	54	16	30
medium GD	64	14	22
team-based	64	19	17

As shown in Table 3.10, in most organisations the groups have leaders. Organisations with leaderless groups are a minority of some 20-plus per cent. In addition, in team-based organisations, the teams are more likely to have leaders than in organisations with weak GD. A possible explanation is that team-based organisations depend more strongly on teams and feel that proper team management requires clear leadership. In addition, virtually all the literature stresses that team leaders must meet high demands. Not only should they be well-informed about the technicalities of the work processes, but social, managerial and leadership skills are also vital for them to function well within a team and organisation. Clearly, people who satisfy such requirements are hard to find and replace and it takes considerable time to acquire the desired skills.

Yet if the ideal of leaderless teams persists on a large scale in practice (the EPOC survey contains no data on this), the high use of team leaders in team-based organisations can also be interpreted as a transitory stage which takes a long time to pass, given that building 'real' teams takes considerable time.

Note also that the term 'team leader' can have vastly different meanings. A team leader might be a *'primus inter pares'*, having the same formal rights and tasks as the group, yet being responsible for the proper functioning of the group processes. He/she can also be the spokesman of the group, doing exactly the same job as all other group members, but also acting as formal interface between group and management. In other cases, the team leader acts as the conventional foreman and takes the decisions for the group. Thus, at one extreme, team leaders are merely supervisors, yet with a different and currently more fashionable job title. Thus, the question about the existence and the choice of a team leader gives us only limited information about the actual decision-making structures within the groups.

A related issue is who chooses the team leader.

Table 3.11 *Different forms of GD by who decides on group leadership (N = 949; row percentages)*

	management	both	group
weak GD	61	23	16
medium GD	57	27	16
team-based	57	25	18

As shown in Table 3.11, in the majority of cases appointing team leaders is a managerial prerogative. In about one fourth of all cases the team and managers jointly decide who are to become team leaders whereas in less than 20% the teams appear autonomous in who they select. The difference between the three different kinds of GD organisations is negligible.

Comparing Tables 3.9 and 3.11, i.e. on the issues of team member selection and leader choice, shows that groups are more likely to (co-)decide who is to become a team member than who is to be team leader. However, the difference between the two tables lies in a shift from joint decision making, in the case of selecting team members, to the managerial prerogative, in the case of choosing leaders.

Further analyses revealed that in most cases, and irrespective of GD form, the same party or parties decide who is to become a team member or team leader. For instance, if the selection of team members is a joint decision of management and the group, in the vast majority of cases they also jointly decide on who is to become team leader. The next most popular option (in about 17% of all cases) is that management decides who is to be team leader, while choosing team members is a joint decision.

Training

Training has always been an important topic for managers and public policy makers. Labels may have changed from '*éducation permanente*' in the 1950s to 'employability' in the 1990s, but the need for training and education continued to feature highly on the agenda. In 1997, the European Commission once again stressed the importance of training in its Green Paper, *Partnership for a New Organisation of Work*. If group delegation is seen as the most advanced option of work organisation, one would assume that it goes along with considerable training efforts. Working together in groups requires cooperative and communicative skills. One can thus presume that introducing forms of collective work creates a need for training in these areas. This not only holds for team members, but also for managers, as other ways of steering people are thought to become necessary when teamworking is introduced. To what extent is training actually provided? Table 3.12 contains data on the extent of training for employees.

We found that relatively little training takes place. Even in the team-based cases, the score stays below one third of organisations. However, team-based organisations do score significantly higher than the two weaker GD forms. This can probably be explained by the higher percentage of the workforce involved in GD.

Table 3.12 *Different forms of GD by training of employees (N = 1403; percentages)*

	data collection and analysis	presentation skills	interpersonal skills	group dynamics
weak GD	23	20	15	18
medium GD	26	29	17	22
team-based	27	30	30	33

The differences between the issues are small, certainly in team-based organisations. Data collection and analysis and presentation skills get about as much attention as 'social' skills, i.e. interpersonal skills and group dynamics.

Table 3.13 contains data on the amount of time spent on training.

Table 3.13 *Different forms of GD by length of training period for employees (N = 714; row percentages)*

	1 day	1-5 days	5 days or more
weak GD	47	38	15
medium GD	22	57	21
team-based	15	67	18

The data show that in less than one fifth of the cases does the total amount of training take more than a week. There is a significant difference between the weaker GD and team-based cases. In about two thirds of the latter, training lasts between one and five days whereas in about half of the weaker GD cases, training takes only one day.

The picture for managers, as shown in Table 3.14, differs somewhat from that for employees, as managers receive more training. As with employee training there is a difference between management training in the weak and medium GD, on the one hand, and team-based cases on the other. Within the team-based cases, the different issues feature practically as equally important, whereas in the two weaker GD forms 'presentation skills' are given less prominence.

Table 3.14 *Different forms of GD by training of managers (N = 1403; percentages)*

	data collection and analysis	presentation skills	interpersonal skills	group dynamics
weak GD	26	18	24	22
medium GD	26	24	26	31
team-based	36	35	36	33

The amount of training for managers is shown in Table 3.15.

Table 3.15 *Different forms of GD by length of training period for managers (N = 647; row percentages)*

	1 day	1-5 days	5 days
weak GD	40	45	15
medium GD	17	55	28
team-based	9	58	33

The data on the length of management training show somewhat more pronounced differences between the two weaker and team-based cases than in the case of the employees. In one third of the team-based cases management training takes more than a week. A comparison of Tables 3.13 and 3.15 shows that management training takes longer than employee training. A further comparison of Tables 3.12 and 3.14 demonstrates that with the exception of presentation skills in medium GD, managers get either roughly the same, (most of the time) more training than employees on the four issues. The difference is greatest in the case of interpersonal skills.

Payment systems

For work in general and perhaps for teamwork in particular, remuneration is a much debated and contested issue. Employers' costs are employees' salaries. In the case of teamwork, skill-based payment systems and the use of team bonuses are often prescribed and experimented with. This is a topic of current interest, at least in business publications and among workers and their representatives, but to what extent do payment systems actually change after introducing GD? Table 3.16 contains the EPOC data on this issue.

Table 3.16 *Different forms of GD by changes to the remuneration system after introducing GD (N = 1261; row percentages)*

	change	no change
weak GD	21	79
medium GD	17	83
team-based	20	80

It follows from Table 3.16 that changes in payment systems are the exception rather than the rule. In only one out of every five cases are payment systems changed and there are only minor differences between the GD subcategories.

Table 3.17 contains data on the kind of changes, if any. It must be noted, however, that the total number of respondents here is rather small.

Table 3.17 *Different forms of GD by kind of changes to the renumeration system (N = 237; percentages)*

	weak GD	medium GD	team-based
personal skills	36	33	35
qualifications	19	27	35
bonus for individual attitude	25	29	32
bonus for individual output	39	32	30
bonus for team output	43	42	54
bonus for flexibility	11	23	22
bonus for quality	21	45	35

Bonuses for team output are the most popular. In about 50% of the cases this type of bonus was implemented. Unfortunately, there are no data available on what the relative amount of the bonuses is compared to individual wages. This is an issue which figures in the debates on team remuneration, as small output bonuses may symbolise the cooperative nature of work and stimulate a feeling of belonging to a group, where large bonuses are often criticised for leading to intense peer pressure. Skill-based pay is the second most popular option, used in about 35% of all cases, irrespective of the form.

Overall, more changes take place in team-based cases than in weak and medium GD cases. Possibly this has to do with a high number of experiments among the latter, which do not justify changes to as politically sensitive an issue as reward structures.

Finally, there are marked differences between countries, as shown in Table 3.18.

Table 3.18: *Changes in payment systems after introducing GD in different countries (N = 1530; row percentages)*

	Yes	No
Denmark	22	78
France	18	82
Germany	15	86
Ireland	14	86
Italy	33	67
Netherlands	11	89
Portugal	6	94
Sweden	28	72
United Kingdom	11	89
Average	19	81

Note: Spain has been omitted due to the small number of workplaces with group delegation in this country (33 workplaces).

Payment systems are changed most often in Italy and Sweden, whereas in the Netherlands and the United Kingdom changes are relatively rare. There is no single explanation for these differences, as probably in every country a country-specific set of factors play a joint role. More generally, existing payment systems may leave considerable room for manoeuvring so that the system does not need to be changed. This appears to be the case in the Netherlands where the widely used function classification and remuneration systems can generally accommodate a change from jobs to qualifications as the basis for remuneration. Elsewhere, regulations may either be so constrained that little change is possible within the system, or alternatively, classification and remuneration systems are hardly used and little is regulated, so that 'anything goes'.

Improvement activities

In the EPOC survey a distinction was made between group consultation and group delegation. The phenomenon of 'quality circles' or project groups, i.e. temporary groups of employees who discuss possibilities of improving work processes, has been treated as a form of group consultation. Such quality circles or project groups may be composed of members from different departments and dissolved after the topic of discussion has been resolved. The outcome is generally advice (or 'suggestions') to management, who can decide whether or not to follow up on that advice for improvement.

In theory, permanent teams of shopfloor employees are in an ideal position to form quality circles as well. In Table 3.7, it was already shown that the right to take decisions in improving work processes is often assigned to the groups (overall in about half of the cases, and 75% in team-based organisations). Team members are experts on the work processes covered by the team, and hence are in a good position to come up with suggestions for improvements. Institutionalising improvement activities within teams, by assigning them responsibility for this, then becomes a plausible option. In this case, the basic permanent work unit coincides with the quality circle which is, indeed, a normal case in Japan. When necessary, outside experts can be added to bring in the required specialist knowledge for the problem at hand. In the EPOC terminology, group consultation and delegation are combined, but such a combination is not necessary. An underlying idea of the central notion of 'autonomy' in sociotechnically-inspired work teams is indeed to facilitate them to come up with improvements. Yet, in the original sociotechnical conceptions, such improvement activities have never been institutionalised, as they have in the Japanese concept of the 'quality circle'. Continuous improvement in Japanese quality circles is strongly guided, both with respect to the pressure on employees to participate and the stress on continuously revising standard operating procedures ('SOPs'). Both these elements are often seen as being at odds with the sociotechnical emphasis on employee autonomy, although that is not necessarily the case. SOPs may constrain employees, but also enable them to act (cf. Adler and Borys, 1996).

Whereas the EPOC survey data do not allow the resolution of the complex theoretical discussions on how quality circles and autonomous work teams relate to each other, against this background it remains interesting to what extent proposals for improvement are combined with group delegation. Table 3.19 contains the answers to the question: 'Does the group propose changes in the organisation and/or planning of work?'

Table 3.19 *Different forms of GD by frequency of proposed changes in the organisation and/or planning of work (N = 1269; row percentages)*

	Changes proposed			
	frequently	sometimes	rarely	never
weak GD	16	60	15	9
medium GD	23	59	12	6
team-based	21	72	7	0

So we find that in about 20 % of all cases, and with little variation between the GD forms, group delegation coincides with frequent suggestions to improve the organisation and/or planning of work. In the vast majority of cases, however, there is just the odd suggestion for improvement. This indicates that in most cases continuous improvement, as far as these aspects are concerned, is not systematically linked to teams.

Table 3.20 shows who decides whether proposed changes are actually implemented.

Irrespective of GD form, the decision whether or not to implement changes is hardly ever left to employees alone. That is not necessarily an indication of a low degree of autonomy, however. In general it suggests that changes may have consequences beyond the work domain of a particular team and hence those 'others' need to be involved. That may explain the high scores for 'management' taking the decisions itself. Only in the case of team-based organisations is joint decision making the most frequently mentioned option.

Table 3.20 *Different forms of GD by who decides whether or not to implement changes (N = 967; row percentages)*

	management	both	group
Weak GD	58	33	9
Medium GD	58	38	4
Team-based	42	53	5

In Table 3.7, it was shown that groups are often given the right to improve their work processes. The same holds for scheduling and allocating work. Combining those findings with the data in Tables 3.19 and 3.20 makes the picture more complex. Apparently, proposals about the planning and/or organisation of work are made less often than those about work processes. This implies that the topics on which groups make suggestions are rather limited, namely that they are restricted to their own work. In this respect, a further analysis showed that if groups are given the decision right to improve work processes, the frequency with which suggestions are made increases, and, in addition, joint decision-making about implementation occurs more often. However, it was found that the effects of these are small.

Conclusions

As the majority of core employees work in groups with more than three decision rights, less than 4% of the workplaces in the survey were categorised as 'team-based'. It could be said, therefore, that the word 'unused' in this report's title overstates the case because of the way missing answers, in the survey responses, have been treated. Nevertheless, these responses show that the application of group work is modest and group delegation is in its infancy in European workplaces.

Contrary to the view one may get from popular and academic literature, manufacturing lags behind in the application of groups – the non-profit sector is a leader and when labour costs are more important, groups are applied more intensively. As already shown in Chapter 2, the number of organisations in which groups with considerable decision-making latitude are the common form of work organisation – team-based organisations – are very much in a minority.

Groups' decision rights are limited, with a clear hierarchy in the topics about which groups may take decisions:

1. allocation of work, scheduling of work, and improving work processes;
2. quality of work, time keeping, and co-ordination; and
3. attendance and absence control, and job rotation.

In the majority of cases, appointing team leaders is a managerial prerogative. Joint decision-making on this issue occurs in only about one fourth of all cases. In slightly more organisations, group members may decide who are to become their colleagues. Training to work in groups occurs in about 20% of the GD organisations and managers are trained slightly more than group members. Payment systems change little, although this is less so in Italy and Sweden. Only in a few cases do systematic improvement activities appear to be integrated with group work. Generally, suggestions for improvement are restricted to employees' work process and hardly ever concern the organisation of a group's work.

The EPOC survey findings show a very bleak picture as they indicate that 'team-based' work organisation in European workplaces is hardly realised.

Chapter 4

Motives for and Effects of Group Delegation

Arguably the most contentious topic in academic and practitioners' discussions on work teams concerns their benefits and merits. Advocates of work teams have always stressed their economic advantages, their greater responsiveness to changing environmental demands and the decrease in absenteeism and sick leave. Increased output volume and better product quality are attributed to and expected from work teams. Besides such economic advantages to organisations, it is claimed that employees benefit, as well, through increased latitude in decision making and hence less stressful work, broader job content, less alienation and improved relationships at work. 'Teams are good for organisations and their members' is the message of team proponents.

Whether this message was believed is another matter. Up until the mid-1980s, it seems as if managers were only inclined to implement teams in times of labour market scarcity, as one of a range of measures to improve the 'quality of working life' in order to make working at their particular company more attractive than a job elsewhere. Teams proclaimed that improvements in the quality of working life made them popular among academic 'action researchers' and some employee representatives. Their engagement may have contributed to a managerial view of teams as 'being nice for people, but not for organisations', and to the perception that essentially teams are about improving the quality of working life, with the claims about their economic benefits being no more than a rhetorical strategy to get them accepted. Troublesome experiences with change processes to get teams implemented may also have reinforced such beliefs.

The rise of Japan as an economic power and the role attributed to shop floor teams in much of the literature on Japan's economic success may have made teams more acceptable to managers – 'if the competitive Japanese use teams, this work organisation must indeed have substantial economic benefits', appears to have become a widely accepted belief. However, it remains unclear how the Japanese 'teams' (cf. Nomura and Jürgens, 1995) compare to European traditions in designing teamwork (Benders and Van Hootegem, 1999). The fact that both are called 'teams' may have led to confusion among practitioners.

The quintessential issues remain. Why do managers implement teams? What motives do they have? Is it for quality of working life, or do they have productivity reasons? What effects do they attribute to teams? Finally, do teams live up to expectations?

Such matters are of prime importance, as managers, like other people, are driven by their beliefs about the efficiency of actions rather than by external 'objective' accounts of the 'real world'.

Motives

The EPOC survey attempted to find the answers to the motives for implementing GD. The possible range of answers have been categorised as follows:

- indicators of productivity
    - the need to improve quality of product or service
    - pressure to reduce cost
    - pressure to reduce throughput time
- quality of working life (QWL)
    - belief that employees have the right to participate
    - desire to improve the quality of working life
- examples elsewhere in the organisation or other organisations
- demands from employees or employee organisations
- the requirements of legislation or collective agreement.

Motives for and Effects of Group Delegation

Table 4.1 presents data on how often these different motives were mentioned.

Table 4.1 *Different forms of GD by motives for introducing group delegation (N = 1404; percentages)*

	productivity	quality of working life	examples elsewhere	legislation/ regulations	employee demands
weak GD	88	48	12	5	9
medium GD	87	70	20	10	12
team-based	83	81	21	13	13
overall	87	64	18	9	11

Overall, productivity is the most important motive for introducing GD. Irrespective of the three forms of GD, five out of six respondents answer that economic motives were relevant. Remarkably, in team-based organisations productivity is mentioned less often as a motive for introducing GD than in weak and medium GD organisations.

In team-based organisations quality of working life is mentioned almost as much as productivity: (81% versus 83%). In the case of weak GD, there is a significant gap between the frequencies with which productivity and the quality of working life are mentioned: (88% versus 48%). Medium GD scores closer to team-based, yet the gap between the two categories of motives is still 17%. Regulative considerations and employee demands are only mentioned in about 10% of all cases. More important are 'examples elsewhere'. Apparently, organisational decision makers watch each other closely, and adoption of group delegation in other organisations may either be an inspiration or make organisations fear lagging behind their competitors if they do not 'go with the flow' (cf. DiMaggio and Powell, 1983).

Table 4.2 contains data on the combinations of the two main motives, productivity and quality of working life.

Table 4.2 *Different forms of GD by combinations of motives for introducing group delegation (N = 1402; row percentages)*

	productivity	quality of working life	both	neither
weak GD	45	4	44	7
medium GD	25	7	62	6
team-based	10	8	72	9
overall	29	6	58	7

The table reveals that quality of working life is hardly even mentioned as the sole reason to introduce teams. If quality of working life is important, then it is generally in combination with economic motives. Productivity alone, i.e. without also mentioning quality of working life, is far more important than just quality of working life. The combination of these two motives, however, occurs most often.

There is also a marked effect of team category. In 72% of the team-based cases, as opposed to only 44% of the weak GD cases, the combination of productivity and QWL motives was found. It is striking that in only 10% of team-based cases was productivity mentioned as the only motive, against 45% in the case of weak GD.

The conclusions are clear:

1. teams are predominantly introduced for productivity reasons;
2. when quality of working life is mentioned as a motive, this generally coincides with productivity; and
3. the combination of quality of working life and productivity occurs more often the more intensive the use of teamwork is.

Apparently, managers have come to believe in the economic advantages of teams, and these beliefs become the driving force to use teams. This is not to say that quality of working life is lost sight of as this motive is often mentioned in combination with productivity.

As indicated in the introduction to this chapter, the developments and traditions on work and organisation design in different European countries are widely varying. QWL has been the focus of much research in Scandinavian countries and in Germany. Here, as well as in France, government-sponsored programmes are meant to ameliorate working life. Advocates of autonomous teamwork were often driven by the prospect of the possibility of improving QWL, together with business performance. One wonders whether such activities had an impact on motives for introducing GD, or whether, perhaps, differences in national values influence the pattern of motives. Table 4.3 contains data on the motives for introducing GD according to the respondents in different countries.

The extent to which respondents mentioned QWL-related and economic motives together does, indeed, differ by country. In the Netherlands (61%), and to a lower degree in three other countries in north-west Europe (Denmark 53%,

Germany 52% and Sweden 51%) the score is above 50%, whereas elsewhere it falls below this mark. The difference between France and the United Kingdom, on the one hand, and the subgroup Denmark, Germany and Sweden, on the other, is small, however. The Irish, in particular, score very low, with only 33% of the Irish respondents mentioning both QWL and economic reasons as motives. This low score is mirrored in the high Irish score in the 'neither' category: (46%). (Of the remaining 54% in Ireland, about 60% mention both QWL and economic reasons).

Table 4.3 *Combinations of motives for introducing group delegation in different countries (N = 1955; row percentages)*

	quality of working life	productivity	both	neither
Denmark	15	10	53	22
France	6	16	49	30
Germany	6	23	52	19
Ireland	4	17	33	46
Italy	3	42	43	12
Netherlands	7	13	61	19
Portugal	3	26	53	19
Sweden	11	19	51	19
United Kingdom	7	26	48	20
Average	8	20	50	22

Note: Spain has been omitted due to the small number of workplaces with group delegation in this country (33 workplaces).

Economic reasons *per se* are clearly more important than QWL, with the exception of Denmark where 15% mentioned QWL as a single motive versus 10% for economic reasons. The latter are clearly most important to Italian organisations (42%), followed by their British counterparts (26%). Except for the Danes, QWL is mentioned most (relatively) often by Swedish respondents (11%).

Depending on one's starting position these data can be interpreted in different ways. When one starts from the notion of 'homogeneity' one can stress that most European countries score fairly similarly as about half of the respondents mention both QWL and economic reasons as motives for introducing GD. Yet there is also heterogeneity, of which examples are pointed out above. These may have to do with the intensity of specific characteristics of national discussions on work and organisation design and the actors involved in these debates.

Effects

The effects can be categorised as follows:

- **Indicators of economic performance:**
  - cost reduction
  - reduction of throughput time
  - improvement of quality of product or service
  - increase in output.
- **Indicators of indirect labour costs:**
  - decrease in sickness
  - decrease in absenteeism.
- **Labour market or employment indicators:**
  - reduction in number of employees ('downsizing')
  - reduction in number of managers.

(Note that the last four effects have an economic as well as a social dimension).

Economically, decreasing levels of absenteeism and sickness mean a larger net utilisation of the factor 'labour' and hence lower labour costs. Furthermore, if total output stays at least at the same level, a smaller workforce means a higher labour productivity. Higher attendance rates are also often used as indications for an improved quality of working life.

The reduction of the workforce can be seen as negative in the short run, but the resulting improved competitiveness may turn out to have a positive employment effect in the longer run. Finally, the reduction of managers may be, but is not necessarily, related to delayering.

Tables 4.4, 4.5 and 4.6 contain data, respectively, on economic performance; indirect labour costs; and employment effects. The category 'Other DP' in these tables serves as a reference point to put the responses into perspective.

Quality improvement clearly scores highest, with percentages over 90%, followed by reduction of throughput time, cost reduction and increasing output volumes.

Table 4.4 *DP workplaces without GD and different forms of GD workplaces by reported economic effects of the introduction of direct participation (N = 5525; percentages)*

	reduction of costs	reduction of throughput time	quality improvement	increase of output
other DP	63	63	92	44
weak GD	67	79	94	52
medium GD	62	59	93	58
Team-based	70	79	96	81

'Team-based' consistently has the highest score. (Only for 'reduction of throughput time' is there an *ex aequo* with weak GD.) Especially on 'increase of output' the difference is considerable. It is remarkable that medium GD's score on the first two indicators falls between the scores of weak GD and team-based and, indeed, scores even lower than 'other DP' for reduction in costs.

Table 4.5 *DP workplaces without GD and different forms of GD workplaces by reported effects of the introduction of direct participation on indirect labour costs (N = 5525; percentages)*

	decrease in sickness	decrease in absenteeism
other DP	33	34
weak GD	36	35
medium GD	33	38
team-based	48	52

As shown in Table 4.5 attendance rates improve with percentages varying between 33% and 52%. This is caused both by decreased sickness rates and by lower absenteeism caused by reasons other than sickness, which are about equally important. With respectively 48% and 52%, team-based organisations score significantly higher than the other GD and DP forms. Apparently, large-scale and (relative) intensive use of group delegation has a markedly positive effect on attendance.

It was also investigated whether assigning the group the decision right to control its attendance has an effect on absenteeism. One would expect that group control over attendance would lead to lower absenteeism, but no relationship was found between these variables.

Compared to the effects on economic performance and, to a smaller extent, on indirect labour costs, the reported effects on employment are modest, yet nevertheless significant. With respect to 'reduction in employees', there is little variation in the scores of the different forms. For the reduction in managers, the story is different. GD has a larger effect than 'other DP' and a reduction in managers is, at 44%, most often reported for team-based workplaces. Only in the latter is a reduction in managers reported more often than a reduction in employees. Given that team members have relatively more decision rights in team-based organisations and that attendance is highest, such results might have been expected. That does not hold true for the fact that reductions in employees and managers are reported more often with weak GD than with medium GD.

Table 4.6 *DP workplaces without GD and different forms of GD workplaces by reported employment effects of the introduction of direct participation (N = 5525; percentages)*

	reduction in no. of employees	reduction in no. of managers
other DP	29	19
weak GD	37	30
medium GD	30	24
team-based	32	44

Table 4.7 contains more data about the reduction in managers, or more specifically, about the relationship between the flattening of organisational structures as a strategic policy initiative, and the reduction in managers as a reported effect.

Table 4.7 *DP workplaces without GD and different forms of GD workplaces by (a) reduction in number of managers as reported effect of the introduction of direct participation and (b) flattening of management structures as strategic initiative (N = 1684; percentages)*

| | reduction in managers ||
	reported effect, not initiative	strategic initiative
other DP	10	39
weak GD	15	53
medium GD	17	33
team-based	36	50

The data show that the number of managers may decline without implementing group delegation. *Vice versa*, a reduction in managers may occur even if it was not an explicit goal. Both have an effect of their own. In GD organisations a reduction in managers is reported more often than in organisations with only other forms of direct participation. This could be expected given that in these organisations groups have more decision rights and hence managers do not need to take these decisions. Another possible reason is that not all groups have leaders. It is not clear, however, whether the respondents consider group leaders as managers.

It is remarkable to note the relatively high proportion (36%) of team-based organisations that report a reduction in managers, even though the latter was not mentioned as a strategic initiative. However, in section 3.3 it was shown that team-based organisations often have team leaders. GD can be a means to decrease the number of hierarchical levels, but that does not necessarily mean that groups operate without leaders.

At first sight, these results are easily one-sidedly interpreted as 'direct participation leads to unemployment'. Indeed, an article in the *Financial Times* based on the first presentation of our survey results singled out this particular issue from a great many other possible topics (Cramb, 1997). However, whether DP is good or bad for employment is not easy to establish. The debate is similar that on the introduction of new forms of technology: job losses may occur, due to more efficient ways of working, but these in turn are likely to enhance an organisation's competitive position, leading to employment gains in the longer run.

Question 16 in the questionnaire allowed us to assess how changes in employment differed between non-users and users of DP. It was formulated as follows: 'How does the number of employees in the largest occupational group compare to three years ago?'

Table 4.8 *Workplaces without DP, DP workplaces without GD and different forms of GD-workplaces by change in employment of largest occupational group (N = 5079; row percentages)*

	increased	same	reduced
non-DP	24	41	35
other DP	34	39	27
weak GD	39	39	22
medium GD	34	44	22
team-based	41	36	23
Overall average	32	40	28

As shown in Table 4.8, the number of respondents that report increased employment is higher among DP users than among non-users, whereas the latter more often report a loss of employment than the former. In combination with the data reported above, this indicates that whereas DP may lead to reduced employment due to more efficient ways of working, this increased efficiency enhances organisations' performance, which has a positive medium-term employment effect.

This line of reasoning also applies for the difference between GD and other DP forms. The GD forms report more increases and less reductions than 'other DP', while between the three forms of GD the differences are slight.

Conclusions

Motives for introducing group delegation are predominantly economic. Organisations introduce it because they think their economic performance will benefit. Quality of working life is also mentioned as a motive, yet generally together with productivity motives. This is strongest in northern Member States. Examples in other organisations have some influence as well, whereas regulations or employee demands are hardly ever reported as motives.

The reported effects seem to indicate that managers should not be disappointed. The reported economic effects are significant and are stronger the more intensely GD is applied. Attendance is reported to have improved as well, which is probably also an indicator of improved quality of working life. The reported employment effects are smallest. Introducing GD leads to less employment for managers and employees. However, the improved economic performance (both direct and as a result of increased labour efficiency) appears to enhance organisations' competitive position, as evidenced by the more positive development of employment in organisations with GD than in organisations with other forms of direct participation or without DP.

Chapter 5

Group Work in an International Perspective

Hitherto, the discussion about the use of group work in different countries can be aptly summarised as much debate based on little data. Trist and Bamforth's (1951) study in a UK mine is generally seen as the start of scholarly attention to autonomous teams, and via Norway, similar ideas came to be applied in Sweden in the 1970s. In the 1980s, in particular, large-scale government-sponsored research programmes paid considerable attention to *Gruppenarbeit* in Germany, but the diffusion of the results appears to have been extremely limited (Latniak, 1995). Only a few publications in English have appeared on the Southern European countries, making these something of a *terra incognita* in the mainstream international literature. In short, in particular countries during certain periods there have been waves of attention to group working, yet it remains uncertain what impact this has had on the actual application of group work. Even in an earlier phase of the EPOC project, an extensive review of empirical literature in different EU member countries, the United States and Japan, had to conclude with respect to making international comparisons:

> we cannot answer these questions on the basis of available research. [...] the research is characterised by extreme diversity: in the problems investigated, methods applied and the depth of measurement and analysis. (Fröhlich and Pekruhl, 1996: 188)

Within the methodological limitations outlined in Chapter 2, the EPOC survey is the first study which allows a comparison of the diffusion of group delegation in the ten European countries investigated. The diffusion of a phenomenon, such as group work, cannot be caught by a single indicator. In Table 5.1, different indicators are presented which together allow the drawing of some conclusions about cross-national differences in the diffusion of group work.

Table 5.1 contains the cross-national data on the use of direct participation, the use of group delegation and the use of the different GD forms as percentages of all workplaces.

Table 5.1 *Workplaces with direct participation and workplaces with (different forms of) group delegation by country (percentages of all workplaces per country)*

	direct participation N = 5786	group delegation N = 2067	different GD forms		
			weak GD	medium GD	team-based
Denmark	81	30	5	21	4
France	87	40	9	24	7
Germany	81	31	12	14	5
Ireland	85	42	8	29	5
Italy	82	28	16	11	1
Netherlands	90	48	10	31	7
Portugal	61	26	5	11	10
Spain	65	7	–	–	–
Sweden	89	56	9	33	14
United Kingdom	83	37	11	19	7

Note: The percentages of the different GD forms for Spain are not included as the total number of GD workplaces is too small for further breakdowns (33 observations). The data for Portugal should be interpreted with care since the number of observations is relatively small (77 workplaces).

The extent to which DP is practised differs by country. Portugal and Spain are clearly at the low end, with 61% and 65% respectively. In contrast, the Netherlands (90%) and Sweden (89%) have the highest levels of practice, with France occupying the third position (87%). All other countries are fairly close to the European average of 81%.

The ranking for GD shows a roughly similar pattern. Spain and Portugal score lowest, although with 7% Spain scores significantly lower than Portugal (26%). The Portuguese score is close to that of Italy (28%), Denmark (30%) and Germany (31%). All these scores fall below the European average of 36%. Once again the Netherlands and Sweden are at the top, yet with 56% Sweden scores higher on the use of GD than the Netherlands (48%), followed by Ireland (42%), France (40%), and the United Kingdom (37%).

Group Work in an International Perspective

The last three columns of Table 5.1 hold data on the incidence of the three GD forms in nine countries – in Spain, there were only 33 GD cases in total, which is too small a sample to measure the three GD forms. The breakdown by GD forms generates a somewhat complex picture. Sweden remains at the top with 14% of team-based workplaces (see last column). The second highest percentage (10%) is for Portugal. However, it must be noted that the number of Portuguese GD cases is small (77) and, therefore, has to be interpreted with care. After these, three countries, France, the Netherlands and the United Kingdom each have a score of 7%. The value of these equal scores is put into some perspective by considering the data in Table 5.2.

Table 5.2 *Different GD forms as percentage of GD workplaces by country (N = 1529; row percentages)*

	weak GD	medium GD	team-based
Denmark	17	71	12
France	23	60	17
Germany	39	46	15
Ireland	18	70	12
Italy	59	38	3
Netherlands	21	65	14
Portugal	20	42	38
Spain	–	–	–
Sweden	17	58	25
United Kingdom	30	50	20

Note: The percentages of the different GD forms for Spain are not included as the total number of GD workplaces is too small for further breakdowns. The data for Portugal should be interpreted with care since the number of observations is relatively small (77 workplaces).

As in Table 5.1, Table 5.2 contains data on the incidence of GD-forms, but it is presented as a percentage of GD workplaces in the countries. This shows, for example, that the percentage of GD workplaces in the Netherlands in higher than in the UK, whereas both countries score equally in team-based cases. One can conclude from this that if British organisations apply group work, it is relatively more often (20%) in the most intensive form, at least compared to the Netherlands (14%). To complicate matters further, the British score on 'weak GD' is also higher than the Dutch, both in absolute (11% versus 10%) and relative (30% versus 21%) terms.

The Swedish (relative) score of 25% remains high, although it is below the Portuguese 38%. Yet, as stated above, the total number of Portuguese GD cases

47

is low. Italy is at the bottom of both tables, followed by Denmark. Germany and Ireland both score 5% on team-based organisations, yet because Irish organisations apply group work more than their German counterparts, the Irish score on team-based cases, as a percentage of GD cases, is lower.

If one were to make a listing of the diffusion of GD based on the various indicators, Sweden should clearly be at the top. The country scores highest on GD and is in the top on 'team-based' workplaces. The Netherlands occupy a clear second place in the application of GD (and score also high on DP in general). At the bottom are Italy, Portugal and Spain, in that sequence.

In between, one can distinguish two groups of countries whose scores are fairly close together: France, Ireland and the United Kingdom score above average in the use of GD, where the Danish and German scores are below average. Within the first group the differences are small: France scores highest on DP, Ireland on GD, whereas the French and British scores (both 7%) on team-based cases are higher than that for Ireland (5%). On the other hand, weak GD scores highest in the UK and lowest in Ireland. The rather low scores of British organisations on all indicators, except 'team-based' as a percentage of all workplaces, means that the UK is placed lowest within this group. The differences between France and Ireland are so small that an *ex aequo* appears apt.

Denmark and Germany have the same score on DP while the difference on GD is small. Somewhat larger is the difference between the Danish and German scores on 'team-based' organisations: (12% and 15% respectively), yet the Danes score lower on weak GD than the Germans. Again, an *ex aequo* appears apt.

Taking all these various scores in combination, it is interesting to note from this analysis that some expectations are confirmed. The low scores for the southern European countries confirm the often held view of lower levels of workplace delegation. The high scores for Sweden and the Netherlands may have to do with the long-standing sociotechnical traditions which directly or indirectly influenced managerial thinking on work organisation. The clear position of Sweden as the top ranking GD country may also have to do with the favourable climate over several decades (Cole, 1985). The Netherlands have also seen a variety of initiatives by academics and practitioners to stimulate organisational forms that incorporate participative workplace arrangements, yet there is no clear dominant infrastructure promoting DP.

The third position of France is somewhat surprising. Perhaps the development of French work organisation deserves more attention in the English language literature than has hitherto been the case. Given the often rather sharp and critical tone of British scholarly publications on teamwork, the third position of the UK is remarkable. The deep economic crisis of the 1970s and 1980s, followed by the advent of foreign investors, large-scale experiments and change programmes with all kinds of 'new forms of work organisation', have apparently had a large impact on British industries. A similar comment must be made for Ireland, as the large influx of foreign investors is likely to have had an influence on forms of work organisation in this country.

It is remarkable that a low use of GD is reported for Denmark and Germany. One might assume that Swedish work practices would have influenced Danish managers, given their Scandinavian links, while in Germany, it would appear that neither the long-standing research programmes nor the hype around 'lean management' in the first half of the 1990s have contributed to a widespread diffusion of GD.

Chapter 6   Teaming up for Teams?

As the majority of core employees work in groups with more than three decision rights, about 4% of the workplaces in the survey were categorised as 'team-based'. It could be said, therefore, that the word 'unused' in this report's title overstates the case because of the way missing answers, in the survey responses, have been treated. Nevertheless, these responses show that the application of group work is modest, and that group delegation is in its infancy in European workplaces.

Groups' decision rights are limited, with a clear hierarchy in the topics about which groups may take decisions:

- allocation of work, scheduling of work, and improving work processes;
- quality of work, time keeping, and co-ordination;
- attendance and absence control, and job rotation.

Joint decision making in appointing team leaders occurs in only about a quarter of all cases, while the appointment of team leaders is, in most cases, a managerial prerogative. This is true to a lesser extent in deciding who are to become group members. Training to help members work in groups occurs in about 20% of the GD organisations. However, managers are trained more than group members. There is little change to payment systems, although in Italy and Sweden such changes are found more than in the other countries. Only in a few cases do systematic improvement activities appear to be integrated with group work. For example, suggestions for improvement are restricted to employees' work processes and hardly ever concern the organisation of a group's work.

The main conclusion of Chapter 4, on motives and effects, is that respondents feel that group delegation enhances organisational performance. In these terms, group work is felt to be useful. Motives for introducing group delegation are predominantly economic – organisations introduce it because they think their economic importance will benefit. Quality of working life is also often mentioned as a motive, yet generally together with productivity motives. Examples in other organisations have some influence as well, whereas regulations or employee demands are hardly ever reported as motives.

The reported effects seem to indicate that managers do not need to be disappointed, as the reported economic effects are significant and stronger the more intensely GD is applied. Attendance is reported to have improved as well, which could also be considered as an indicator of improved quality of working life. On the reported employment effects, the introduction of GD leads to less employment for managers and employees. However, an improved economic performance (both direct and as a result of increased labour efficiency) benefits the competitive position of organisations, as shown by the more positive development of employment in organisations with GD compared with organisations with other forms of direct participation or without direct participation.

As regards country comparisons, having compared several indicators, Sweden and the Netherlands have the highest levels of group delegation, while France, Ireland and the United Kingdom are above the European average, and Denmark and Germany are just below the average. The three countries in the south – Italy, Portugal and Spain – were found, on the basis of these comparisons, to be at the bottom.

The high ranking of Sweden and the low places of southern European countries confirm earlier expectations. However, it is interesting that in Germany there is a contrast between the intensity of discussions about *Gruppenarbeit*, and the relatively low diffusion of group delegation.

Discussion

After several decades, the abundant research, experiments, pilot projects and dissemination of the acquired knowledge on group work seems to have had an impact on organisational practice in Europe. Because the EPOC data are not longitudinal, from this source alone we cannot be sure that our claim that group working is gradually getting off the ground, if not breaking through, is justified. Yet indications from other sources suggest that this is actually the case. For instance, recent data on the development of group work in Germany reveal that the percentage of the workforce which is employed in groups rose from 6.9% in 1993 to 11.8% in 1998. However, it must be considered that most of the groups still have little autonomy and participation. The number of employees working in a semi-autonomous form of group in this study is still small. It has increased, however, from 2.2% in 1993 to 3.2% in 1998 (Nordhause-Janz and Pekruhl, forthcoming).

For the near future, the focus on productivity motives and the combined realisation of economic and 'quality of working life' effects, as reported in the EPOC survey, lead us to expect that group working will gain additional popularity. If powerful organisational decision makers are actually convinced that groups are good for business, this will prove more influential than any legislative or regulative measures. It is also worth noting that it took decades of sustained attention to group work before this form of work organisation became accepted as important. This underlines the importance of continuing the dissemination of knowledge on team-based working, such as that provided by the EPOC survey data.

With the constant flow of articles highlighting the merits of group work, one might argue that commercial parties have taken over this role and that there is no need for further involvement of other parties, including public authorities. Yet there remains a need to strengthen the existing weak points, such as the low commitment to training, and to provide a balanced account of the advantages and disadvantages of group work.

It should be noted, however, that the apparent increasing popularity of group work may backfire. In the first place, organisations may start jumping on the bandwagon out of fear of lagging behind their competitors or because of a belief in easily gained performance improvements, without a clear idea of what they want to achieve with groups and what consequences group working will have in their particular cases. A possible explanation for the overall low use of group work is provided by the difficulties in the transition from traditional forms of work organisation to groups. Most organisational change projects tend to be cumbersome; this is more likely the more drastic the proposed changes are. Implementing group working arrangements is not easy. It is a development process which often takes years and for which the risks of failure are substantial.

Secondly, there is the issue of autonomy – how far can and should it go? The data show that autonomy for team members in Europe is currently very limited. Yet for every member of an organisation, or indeed of society, full autonomy is an illusion. Nobody lives in a social vacuum, certainly not employees who are supposed to contribute to their organisations' overall commercial goals. Consequently, there will always be some form of organisational control, whether people work in groups or in any other form of work organisation. Group working is thus not a matter of autonomy or control, it is a particular combination of autonomy and control. Stressing the first and denying the last in order to promote groups may backfire when group members come to realise that the first is limited and the latter still exists. Hence, both aspects need to be addressed, so that they can be discussed and/or negotiated.

This concerns, for instance, the existence and choice of team leaders and/or the choice of group members. In addition, devolving control over personnel matters to the group runs the risk of coercive control patterns, internal 'mobbing'. In this sense, autonomy can lead to intense and unregulated intra-team control, reinforced by group bonuses and peer pressure (Sewell, 1998). There is, therefore, the possibility of a 'tyranny of a team ideology' (Sinclair 1992), thereby providing counterweight against the sometimes over-optimistic messages in the managerial literature. The emphasis on economic aspects lends some empirical support to the importance of such concerns from a social point of view, although these are partly counter-balanced by the importance of QWL motives. The potentially negative aspects of group working were only partly covered by the EPOC survey, yet need to be taken seriously both in terms of future research and dissemination of information to practitioners.

A one-sided stressing of the benefits of group work, while at the same time neglecting the potential disadvantages, may in the long run lead to an increasing number of failures, which may give group working a bad reputation. Group work should not wear out through use!

Group work is felt to be useful, but little used.

Policy recommendations

The main conclusion of this report suggests that there is a need to further stimulate group work. If the social partners wish to promote this form of work organisation, there are some lessons to be learnt from the EPOC data.

In the first place, the 'team-worker message' has been repeated constantly during the last five decades, yet throughout most of this period it was not picked up. If difficult organisational innovations, such as group work, are to be diffused, it is necessary to constantly emphasise their potential. Programmes or campaigns that only last a limited number of years seem to have made a small contribution. Endurance is vital, especially if the message is perceived to be 'old', as may easily become the case in a managerial world that is continuously looking for novelties and new approaches.

Secondly, one may choose to stimulate the creation and maintenance of local networks, composed of organisations with experience and an interest in groups, supplemented by external experts, such as researchers or consultants. Such networks may be of particular relevance for small and medium-sized organisations.

Recalling the importance that respondents attached to 'examples elsewhere', the networks should be focused on the exchange of what might be called 'realistic information': practical experiences with groups, including or perhaps even stressing, the more troublesome aspects. Overly optimistic messages ('best practices') about the merits of groups need to be supplemented with or even replaced by realistic accounts, if the risk of backfiring is to be reduced. Any organisational change project has its problems and participants involved in them should be aware of this. Networks can have a function in enabling the implementation and spread of group work.

Thirdly, the potentially negative aspects of groups deserve attention. Employee representatives, labour inspectorates, regulation and legislation may fulfil useful roles here. To avoid misunderstanding, the idea is not to impose group work; such a strategy is unlikely to be effective. Instead, harmful effects need to be prevented or corrected.

Closer involvement of employee representatives may also have a positive effect on the so far rather neglected aspect of training (both for technical and social aspects).

A recommendation for further research concerns the development paths in different European countries. The cross-national comparison in Chapter 5 made clear that 'talking the talk' does not necessarily coincide with 'walking the walk'. Various factors which together influence development patterns have been pointed out (Cole, 1985), but more needs to be known about the relative importance of national discussions on work and organisational design, the different parties involved, their credibility in the eyes of key decision makers and the channels for disseminating knowledge.

Longitudinal research is necessary to get a better view of group work's diffusion over time. Ideally, such research would be aimed at both employees (Kleinschmidt and Pekruhl, 1994; Nordhause-Janz and Pekruhl, forthcoming) and at organisations, as in the EPOC survey, so that the findings might complement each other.

References

Adler, P.S. and B. Borys, 'Two types of bureaucracy: enabling and coercive', *Administrative Science Quarterly*, 40(1), 1996, pp. 61-89.

Benders, J. and G. Van Hootegem, (1999), 'Teams and their context: moving the team discussion beyond dichotomies', *Journal of Management Studies*, 36(5).

Beyerlein, M. (ed.), *Work Teams: Past, Present and Future*, Boston, Kluwer Academic Publishers, 1999.

Brewster, C. and A. Hegewisch (eds.), *Policy and Practice in European Human Resource Management: The Price Waterhouse Cranfield survey*, London, Routledge, 1994.

Buchanan, D., 'An eager and enduring embrace: the ongoing rediscovery of a management idea', in: Procter, S. and F. Mueller (eds.), *Teamworking*, London, Macmillan, 1999.

Cole, R.E., 'The macropolitics of organizational change: a comparative analysis of the spread of small-group activities', *Administrative Science Quarterly*, 30(4), 1985, pp. 560-585.

Cramb, G. (1997), '"Open" companies lead job-loss league', *Financial Times*, (33263), 2.

Czarniawska, B. and B. Joerges (1996), 'Travels of Ideas', in: Czarniawska, B. and G. Sevón (eds.), *Translating Organisational Change*, Berlin/New York, de Gruyter, pp. 13-48.

DiMaggio, P.J. and W.W. Powell, 'The iron cage revisited: institutional isomorphism and collective rationality in organizational fields', *American Sociological Review*, 48(2), 1983, pp. 147-160.

Dore, R., *British Factory – Japanese Factory*, London, Allen and Unwin, 1973.

European Commission, *Partnership for a new organisation of work*, Luxembourg, Office for Official Publications of the European Communities, 1997.

EPOC Research Group, *New forms of work organisation. Can Europe realise its potential? Results of a survey of direct employee participation in Europe*, Luxembourg, Office for Official Publications of the European Communities, 1997.

Fröhlich, D., C. Gill and H. Krieger, *Workplace involvement in technological innovation in the European Community*, volume I: *roads to participation*, Luxembourg, Office for Official Publications of the European Communities, 1993.

Fröhlich, D. and U. Pekruhl, *Direct participation and organisational change: fashionable but misunderstood? An analysis of research in Europe, Japan and the USA*, Luxembourg, Office for Official Publications of the European Communities, 1996.

Geary, J. and K. Sisson, *Conceptualising Direct Participation in Organisational Change. The EPOC Project*, Dublin: European Foundation for the Improvement of Living and Working Conditions.

Harzing, A.-W., 'Response rates in international mail surveys: results of a 22-country study', *International Business Review*, 6(6), 1997, pp. 641-665.

Kleinschmidt, M. and U. Pekruhl, 'Kooperation, Partizipation und Autonomie: Gruppenarbeit in deutschen Betrieben', *Arbeit*, 4(2), 1994, pp. 150-172.

Kovacs, I., C. Cerdeira and A. Brandao Moniz, *Technological and Work Organisational Change in Portuguese Industry*, Lisbon, G.G.I, G.G.T.p.e.Ceso I&D, 1992.

References

Latniak, E., '"Technikgestaltung" (shaping of technology) and direct participation: German experiences in managing technological change', in: Benders, J., J. de Haan and D. Bennett (eds.), *The Symbiosis of Work and Technology*, London//Bristol, Taylor and Francis, 1995, pp. 59-76.

Lay, G., C. Dreher and S. Kinkel, *Neue Produktionskonzepte leisten einen Beitrag zur Sicherung des Standorts Deutschland. Mitteilungen aus der Produktions-innovationserhebung*, Karlsruhe, Fraunhofer Institut Systemtechnik und Innovationsforschung, 1996.

Muffels, R., T. Heinen and G. van Mil, *Werkoverleg en werkstructurering en de subsidieregeling arbeidsplaatsverbetering: En onderzoek bij bedrijven met meer dan 100 personeelsleden*, Tilburg, IVA, 1982.

Nomura, M. and U. Jürgens, *Binnenstrukturen des japanischen Produktivitätserfolges; Arbeitsbeziehungen und Leistungsregulierung in zwei japanischen Automobilunternehmen*, Berlin, Sigma, 1995.

Nordhause-Janz, J. and U. Pekruhl, *Groupwork in Germany* (provisional title), Gelsenkirchen, Institut Arbeit und Technik, forthcoming.

NUTEK, *Towards Flexible Organisations*, Stockholm,, NUTEK, 1996.

Regalia, I., European Foundation for the Improvement of Living and Working Conditions, *Humanise work and increase profitability? Direct participation in organisational change viewed by the social partners in Europe*, Luxembourg, Office for Official Publications of the European Communities, 1995.

Sewell, G., 'The discipline of teams: the control of team-based industrial work through Eelectronic and peer surveilance', *Administrative Science Quarterly*, 42(2), 1998, pp. 397-428.

Sinclair, A., 'The tyranny of a team ideology', *Organization Studies*, 13(4), 1992, pp. 611-626.

de Sitter, L.U., *Synergetisch produceren: human resources mobilisation in de produktie: een inleiding in de struktuurbouw* (second edition), Assen,, Van Gorcum, 1998.

Trist, E.A. and K.W. Bamforth, 'Some social and psychological consequences of the Longwall method of coal-getting', *Human Relations*, 4(1), 1951, pp. 3-38.

van Eijnatten, F.M., *The Paradigm that Changed the Workplace*, Stockholm/Assen,, Arbetslivscentrum\van Gorcum, 1993.

Womack, J.P., D.T. Jones and D. Roos, *The Machine That Changed the World*, New York, Harper Perennial, 1991.

European Foundation for the Improvement of Living and Working Conditions

Useful but Unused – Group Work in Europe

Luxembourg: Office for Official Publications of the European Communities

1999 –60 pp. – 16 x 23.5 cm

ISBN 92-828-5568-6

Price (excluding VAT) in Luxembourg: EUR 20